Olivia Lauren's
OLIVIA CONNECTS
A Guide to Modes of Communication

Melissa-Sue John and Alyssa Simone

Youth Illustrator: Lionel Emabat

Lauren Simone Publishing House

Library of Congress Cataloging-in-Publication Data

John, Melissa-Sue and Simone, Alyssa
Olivia Lauren's Olivia Connects: A Guide to Modes of Communication

Melissa-Sue John and Alyssa Simone
p. cm.
Illustration by Lionel Emabat

Summary: A kid friendly and multicultural approach to learning the different modes of communication. Olivia Connects explores different communication varying in communication style, technology, physical ability, and time period.
ISBN-13: 9780997952056
ISBN-10: 0997952059
Title I. Series (volume 4). Olivia Lauren
1. Verbal and Nonverbal communication 2. Physical challenges 3. Technology

2017909712

Lauren Simone
PUBLISHING HOUSE
www.laurensimonepubs.com

This book belongs to:

_____

Dedication

Janette Rivera for the inspiration.

Alina Dowe, Cheryl Gorham, Matthew John, Andre Kerr, and Janet Reynolds for their feedback.

All of Our Friends who stay connected.
We say Thank You!

TABLE OF CONTENTS

Communication can be *formal* or *informal*. Vera wrote two letters. What are the differences between the two?

Dear Olivia Lauren

I am writing to inform you that I arrived safely. I am sorry you were unable to come.

I will talk to you later.

Sincerely,
Vera

Olivia

I made it. Wish you were here.

TTYL!

Love ya
Vera

Friends
-4-
Ever

Formal communication, often used with teachers or coworkers, is very polite, usually longer, and more professional.

Informal communication, often used with friends or siblings, is relaxed, brief, and sometimes uses slang or acronyms.

Communication can also be written or oral.

Letters are a form of *written communication*. When Vera tells me something verbally, she uses *oral communication*.

As you may have guessed, there are many types of written communication.

newspaper

books

I write *blogs* and send *text messages*. Nelson reads *magazines*. These are all forms of written or typed communication.

My friends talk a lot and I mean a lot. They use so many devices made for oral communication. Rosa *video chats* with Taj using the *computer*, while Adam does the same using his *tablet*. Harriet talks on a *telephone*.

Xavier talks on his *cellphone*, while Nelson uses a *payphone*. Other devices we use are the *radio, television, videogames*, and even, *virtual reality*.

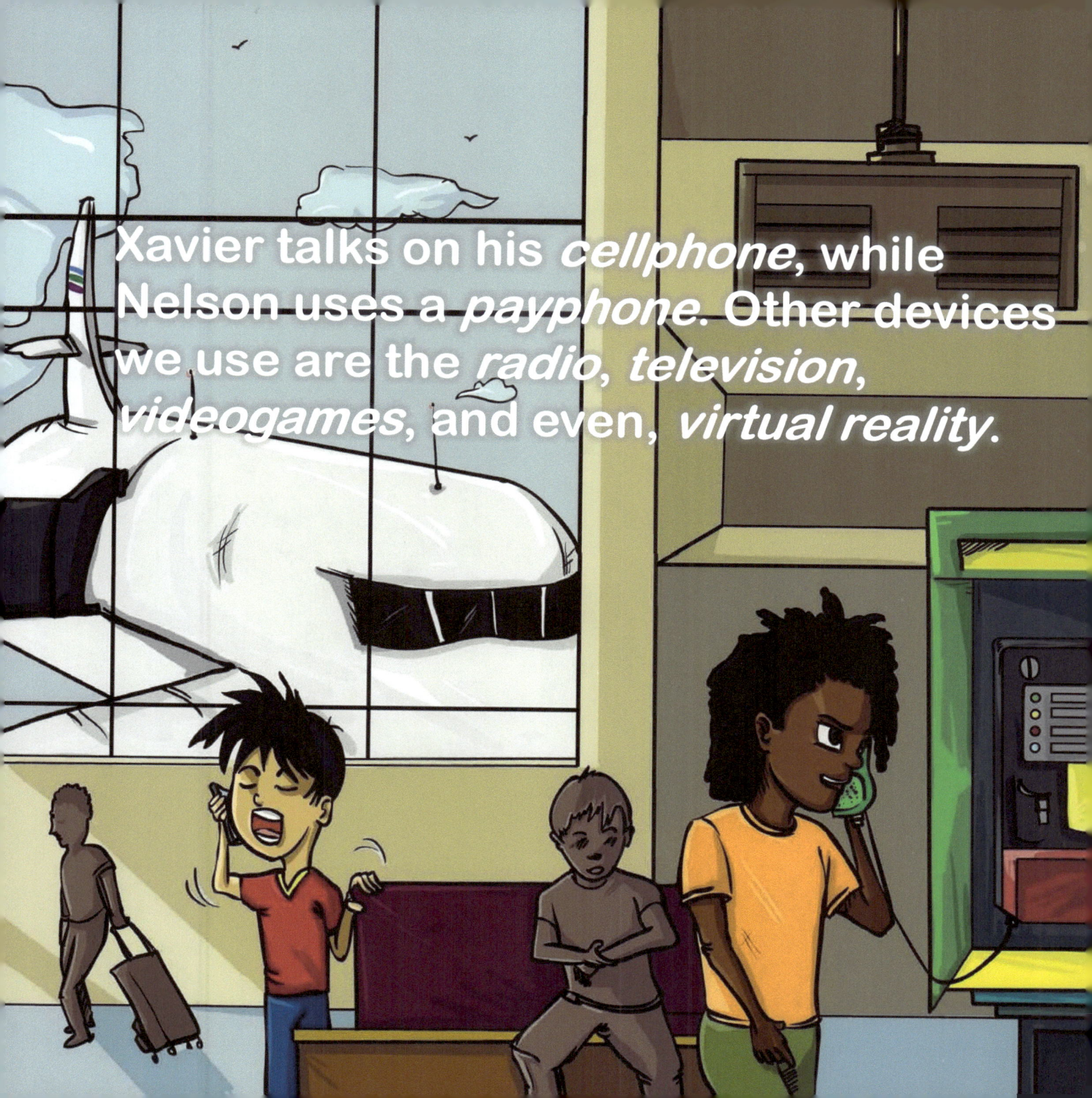

Harriet is headed out with her mom. She waves "hello" to me. This is *nonverbal communication*.

Nelson and Xavier don't always use words to communicate. Reading *body language* is a form of nonverbal communication.

People who can't hear or speak also use nonverbal communication.

Harriet and I are learning *sign language* to communicate with our friends with hearing (deaf or hard-of-hearing) or speech challenges.

Maria has a visual challenge called blindness. She uses *braille* to read.

Jack has cerebral palsy. He uses a device made for nonverbal communication called an *eye tracking device.*

Taj and I wondered how people communicated before the age of technology. The oldest forms of communication were instruments such as *horns* and *trumpets*.

Drums were also used during ceremonies and wars. The sound of the drum energized the soldiers and scared the enemy during battle.

In Ancient Egypt and Ancient Greece, they used drawings called *hieroglyphs* (hi-er-o-glifs) to communicate.

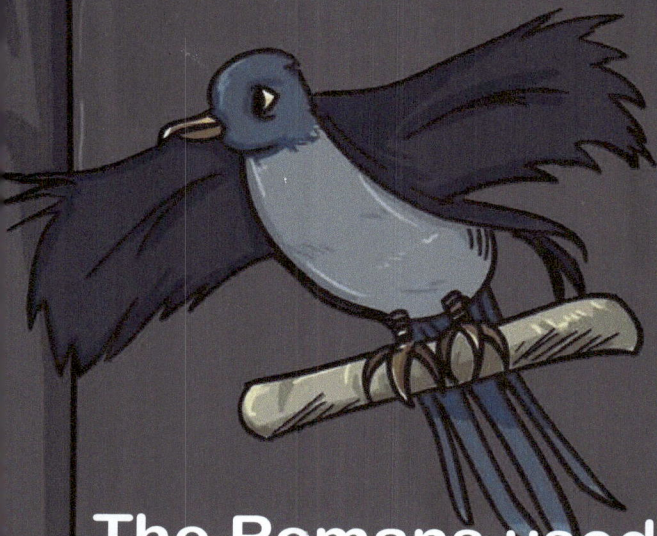

Before paper, they used *papyrus* and scrolls. *Quills*, ink, pens, and pencils were later invented.

Smoke signals were used by Native American tribes to alert each other when they needed help.

The *telegraph* was once the fastest way to send messages. It used electricity to send coded messages through wires to communicate quickly over long distances.

The *typewriter* is a manual machine that has a keyboard, a ribbon made of ink, and a paper roller. When a letter or symbol on the keyboard is pressed, it transfers the ink to the paper.

Glossary

Body Language: Gestures such as movements of hand, head, or body to express an idea or feeling

Braille: A system of raised dots that can be read using fingers of those who cannot see

Cellphone: A mobile phone, short for cellular phone

Communication: A way to send and receive messages

Computers: An electronic tool that stores information

Email: An electronic letter

Formal Communication: Professional ways to share information

Informal Communication: A casual conversations between people socializing

Mute: Unable to use speech

Nonverbal Communication: Communication without speech

Oral Communication: interaction between people talking, sharing ideas and information

Papyrus: Ancient paper made from a tall grass grown in Egypt

Payphone: A public telephone that uses coins or card

Sign Language: Use of hand motions to communicate

Slang: Informal language

Verbal Communication: Use of words to communicate (oral or written)

Written Communication: Communication by handwritten or printed symbols

Video Chat: Communication with picture and sound using phone or computer

Quill: A pen made from the feather of a large bird

Telephone: A telephone used in a home or business

Biographies

Olivia Lauren, whom the main character is based, is a 9 year old, actor, model, and author. Follow on Instagram @olivialaurenj

Alyssa Simone enjoys writing stories, drawing, acting, and modeling. She is a smart, confident, talented teen with great work ethic. She also runs track and plays the violin. Follow @alyssasimonej

Melissa-Sue John, Ph.D. is a psychology professor, mom of two girls, wife, and author of children's literature. She is on a mission to create fun, educational and diverse children's literature, coauthored with young writers and illustrated by young illustrators. Follow @laurensimonepubs

Lionel Emabat considers drawing as more than just a hobby or a gift. For him, it is a lifestyle. Lionel is now a college graduate with B.A. in Digital Design and Illustration. Follow @leo_t22

9 780997 952056